Creative Recognitions, Inc.

Flourish vs. Languish Which Side Are You On?

Creative Recognitions, Inc.

Flourish vs. Languish
Which Side Are You On?

SherryBlairInstitute.com

Copyright © 2016 Sherry A. Blair
SHAKTI PUBLISHING
All rights reserved.

DO NOT DUPLICATE OR DISTRIBUTE WITHOUT WRITTEN PERMISSION. This copyrighted electronic or physical publication is a personal book and is intended exclusively for use by an individual or by individuals in a training program, which is led by a Positivity Pulse Partners facilitator. This book, either electronic or physical, in its whole or any part thereof may not be forwarded or duplicated singly or for use in a classroom or other group setting or online or for use as part of a training program without written permission. Such use may be only be granted by Sherry Blair Institute For Inspirational Change in a written agreement and upon payment of applicable fees. For information on bulk sales or becoming a facilitator please email: info@SherryBlairInstitute.com.

Illustrations by: Brenda Brown
www.webtoon.com

Cover Design and Page Layout by: Kristine Requena

ISBN-13: 978-1490959528
ISBN-10: 1490959521

Accolades for *The Positivity Pulse: Transforming your Workplace* from which this modern fable *Creative Recognitions, Inc.* was excerpted:

★★★★★ 5 out of 5 stars

Spectacular! This book is a must read for anyone looking to make positive changes in the leadership of their organization. Using carefully crafted illustrations the writer is able to tranform the reader into becoming excited about new perspectives that capture the essence of true leadership. Ms. Blair is a skilled and talented writer which makes this book very easy to read while inspiring the reader to make positive changes. I enjoyed this book and highly recommend reading it.

Debbie Riddle, Executive Director

★★★★★ 5 out of 5 stars

A great read and can transform any work place to positivity! A great read and can transform any work place to positivity. I recommend this approach to any workplace that wants to increase employee productivity, recognize their employees' successes, and have employees feel that this is a great place to work at.

Phil Hymowitz, LCSW

★★★★★ 5 out of 5 stars

A Concept Which Will Truly Inspire and Motivate Workers! This book was an excellent read. The Nurtured Heart Approach® will surely continue to gain traction in transforming the workplace. Sherry Blair has done a great job in articulating methods which will guarantee success for any manager willing to apply them. Younger workers (Gen Y) surely will be motivated by this method. The days of managing by fear and focusing on the negative will soon be over.

Gordon Marzano, Human Resources Manager

★★★★★ 5 out of 5 stars

Positively engaging! This book uses fictional characters (who resemble people we all know at work) to illustrate how different attitudes and approaches can either help propel people toward success or pull them down to complacency or worse. The illustrations are great, and the scenarios and examples make the concepts very easy to understand. Anyone who reads this book should come away with a brighter outlook and tools that will make them a more influential leader at work, at home, and everywhere. I highly recommend the book to anyone to cares about morale and engagement in the workplace and who wants to see their company positively transformed.

**Peggy O. Archuleta, RN, BSN, CMSRN, CDE
Banner Estrella Medical Center**

★★★★★ 5 out of 5 stars

A Fantastic Book! I love Sherry Blair's brilliant way of bringing the Nurtured Heart Approach® to the workplace. This book will undoubted catch on like wildfire and will have a wonderfully transformative impact on any business, corporation or organization that chooses to takes it on. Thanks for this fantastic book!!!

Howard Glasser, Creator of The Nurtured Heart Approach®

★★★★★ 5 out of 5 stars

A Must Read! I am a manager in a human service agency. We pride ourselves on having a positive culture and incorporating the latest, best corporate ideology available. Ms.Blair's book is a direct HIT!! The teaching metaphor is simple and the message relevant and powerful. Even as I write I am smiling thinking of the characters. I love the way Ms. Blair incorporates classic corporate thinking and wisdom with the ancient wisdom of the Nurtured Heart Approach®. This book re-energized me, taught me some new things and confirmed the path of HEART focused leadership is the ONLY WAY.

Joe Clem, MA, LMFT
Founder/Center for Marriage & Family

★★★★★ 5 out of 5 stars

BRILLIANT! Sherry Blair has creatively, concisely, and effectively encapsulated the essence and the clarity of The Nurtured Heart Approach® with a focus on the workplace. The allegorical representation of human perspectives and behaviors, and the practical, clear-cut application of Howard Glasser's NHA within the context of Marty Seligman's 'Positive Psychology' is easily graspable, immediately useful, and deeply energizing. Kudos!

Angela R. Smith, CAS, NCC, LPC
A Nurtured Heart Approach® School
Counselor & Coach, Hampton, VA

★★★★★ 5 out of 5 stars

EXCELLENT! This book has transformed the way I look at my job and my workplace! I am working now to increase engagement within my team to this approach. It truly makes working in the office a pleasure if you follow the rules! The book is well written and very succinct. Sherry Blair is a consummate professional with years of experience that she brings to the story. The camera references really bring a picture to the reader, and help cement the ideas that Sherry describes. I have recommended her and her book to my company and I hope the enthusiasm spreads!! Thanks Sherry for such a great read!

Beth Hymowitz, Corporate Sr. Project Manager

Creative Recognitions, Inc.

Flourish vs. Languish Which Side Are You On?

Sherry A. Blair

*Just when the caterpillar thought
the world was over, it became a butterfly.*

—Proverb

In a gorgeous green meadow dotted with wildflowers, the frontline staff of Creative Recognitions, Inc., is hard at work. Their mission: to train corporate leaders in the latest and most effective styles of leadership. At the offices, frontline workers handle scheduling, paperwork, and correspondence. Leadership creates and gives trainings, keeps up to date on the latest in corporate leadership, and manages frontline workers.

Positivity Pulse

Isabella

    Upon first entering the offices of Creative Recognitions, Inc., one sees the smiling face of Isabella. She is flourishing in her job. Coming to work is a joy; she feels supported and appreciated. Work is a place she can grow and change in a positive way. Even as a frontline worker, she understands that the role she fills is just as important as that of the company's CEO. Sure, she makes mistakes and breaks rules, but there's no fallout and no drama. Mistakes are no big deal. She doesn't dwell on what she's done wrong. Instead, she quickly steps back into her greatness.

Creative Recognitions, Inc.

To be continuously bathed in positive feedback, all Isabella needs to do is make her best effort to keep up with her work, follow the rules, and adhere to policy. No wonder she wants to shine! As she continues through her day and works on her project, she turns more and more golden. The silk strands of her chrysalis are beginning to form. She's well on her way to metamorphosis.

Justice

This is Justice. When he makes the effort to do well, he goes through his day hearing comments such as "Thanks!" or "Good job," but he never quite knows why he's being thanked or how he's doing a good job. At the end of each day, he feels as though he's had nothing but junk food to eat—he's had plenty of seemingly positive reinforcement, but he craves more. He never quite feels satiated.

On the other hand, even for smaller infractions of policy or rules, he is given lots of negative attention. Sometimes the higher-ups even call a big meeting to discuss his rule-breaking. Justice feels picked on by his supervisors. Although getting in

Creative Recognitions, Inc.

trouble feels terrible, Justice feels drawn to breaking rules, or to walking that fine line between rules followed and rules broken. It's the only way he gets the attention he craves from leadership and from his frontline peers.

Justice has very few gold stripes on his body, and he hasn't figured out how to begin wrapping himself in the comforting softness of silk. He becomes fearful that he won't make his deadlines. If this happens, he won't be able to move into the next phase of the project.

Sometimes Justice wonders why he even bothers to come to work. He works just as hard as Isabella and his accomplishments are similar to hers, but for some reason she is changing and growing, moving at an astonishingly rapid pace toward project completion—toward metamorphosis. It even seems that she is more liked than Justice. "It's just not fair," Justice grumbles.

Isabella and Justice's fellow frontline workers each fall into one or the other category: progressing toward metamorphosis or stuck in a state of inertia; feeling recognized for even their small successes or as though they can't do anything right; growing and changing rapidly or wanting to metamorphose but not knowing how to begin.

What makes some of these workers grow and flourish while others languish? These differences have a lot to do with the leaders who guide and supervise their work. Ultimately, the responsibility of the company's leadership teams is to guide team members toward the chrysalis stage, even as they themselves accrue golden stripes and build their own chrysalises. Leaders need to fill frontline workers to capacity with the nutrients they require to transform in the final stage, where project completion—metamorphosis—can take place.

Some leadership teams are having greater success with this than others.

Team Chrysalis

Mr. Moody, Mrs. Crabtree, and Mr. Silencio, who supervise Justice and others like him, are members of Team Chrysalis. These leaders have diverse qualities and strengths. Some are new team players and some are seasoned. Their gold stripes are well established and their silk chrysalides are taking shape, but each is stuck in a unique way. Each encounters different kinds of obstacles to imparting their wisdom and greatness to the people in their lives.

Creative Recognitions, Inc.

Mr. Moody

Mr. Moody is a seasoned member of this team. He's close to retirement and has contributed in magnificent ways to the company's sustainable development. Although he regularly thanks his team members and frontline workers for doing a good job, his moods can sometimes make him difficult to get along with. He himself has lots of gold stripes, but for some reason he seems stuck—he has not moved far enough into his own transformation to set a truly inspiring example for Justice, Isabella, and their co-workers.

Mrs. Crabtree

Mrs. Crabtree is task oriented and full of wisdom. But in her role as a team leader, she seems to spend much of the day barking orders and punishing her staff. She has a tendency to lecture when someone does something wrong. Even on a good day, she's abrupt and a bit crabby; she's in a constant state of frustration because she sees around her only employees who are making mistakes! She can't seem to escalate disciplinary

Creative Recognitions, Inc.

actions far enough to have an impact. At the same time, she doesn't ever seem to notice when her fellow team members or frontline workers are shining.

"That's just what I expect from them," she'd likely say if someone asked her why she never gave positive feedback to her team. "They're going to have to do a lot better than this to get a pat on the back from me. Besides, they get a paycheck to do what they were hired to do."

In private moments, Mrs. Crabtree feels unhappy that her gold stripes are barely showing and that her chrysalis is tattered and in need of much more silk before she can enter her own metamorphosis. Like Mr. Moody, she knows that she isn't setting a great example for her fellow leaders or for the followers who count on her for guidance—but she doesn't know how to change to set this example.

Mr. Silencio

Mr. Silencio is the quiet type, but his contributions to the team are nothing less than stellar. He has many gold stripes and has finished his chrysalis in preparation for metamorphosis, but he has not yet begun his transformation in earnest. Although frontline workers and fellow team members learn a great deal from his intellect, he says barely a word to them directly.

Whether they're doing well (which gives him a good feeling) or breaking the rules (which bothers him), he says nothing. His frontline workers have no trouble getting away with rule-breaking when he is around. On the other hand, they don't feel inspired to do a better job, because Mr. Silencio doesn't seem to have a preference or a voice one way or the other. He is stuck in his own chrysalis.

The Nurtured Heart® Warriors Team

Mr. Kodak, Mrs. Polaroid, and Ms. Canon, members of the Nurtured Heart® Warriors Team, believe that creating a brilliant workplace is all about celebrating what's going well. They do not agree with top-down leadership styles, choosing instead to value the voice of every single person who works for the company. Their mission is to nurture personal and professional development—to support everyone into their metamorphosis to greatness. Their transformation into butterflies is complete, and they're ready to show others the way.

Mr. Kodak

This is Mr. Kodak. He seems to notice everything that's going right. Whomever he speaks to comes away feeling special. Even if it's something small—a choice to follow the rules, or just showing up and paying attention—he has something good to say about it. Practically everywhere he goes, Mr. Kodak takes "snapshots" of successes, both miniscule and massive, and he's unfailingly generous when giving feedback to team members about those successes.

Creative Recognitions, Inc.

Mrs. Polaroid

This is Mrs. Polaroid. As a more seasoned manager, she can keep up with Mr. Kodak in terms of noticing and acknowledging success. Like a Polaroid camera, she captures successes as they happen, then deepens that image of success by clearly stating how those successes reveal strengths and virtues. Her unique, intense style takes some getting used to, but in the end, this ability to hone in on what's going right—and on what's so right about it—makes her an invaluable member of the management team.

Ms. Canon

Ms. Canon is the team's ultimate policy implementer and relentless rule follower, but she's not one to lecture, reprimand, or scold when rules are broken. Instead, she recognizes *rule-following*. She keeps the team in full compliance by offering frequent reminders to those staying on task: *you are wonderful for not breaking rules and for following policy*. Ms. Canon appreciates team members for their willingness to change old habits, for staying in healthy control and for re-routing themselves back to compliance when they break rules or fail to comply with company policies and procedures. She's firm and strict, but also compassionate, loving, and proactive.

Creative Recognitions, Inc.

Señora Corazon: CEO

Señora Corazon, CEO of Creative Recognitions, Inc., has been accused of wearing rose-colored glasses. She seems to believe, sometimes beyond reason, that all people can flourish. Her view is that giving recognition for every success, brilliance, and accomplishment is good for everyone, including the one who gives that recognition. She loves to notice what people are doing in the moment—or even what they're wearing!—and to take time to tell them what she's observing. She communicates to her people that she values them for positive attitude and great work ethic.

Even when staff members seem to be having a rough day,

she finds ways to positively acknowledge them for their ability to deal with hard times or difficult tasks. Other leaders have not agreed with her approach. They stand behind traditional ways of ruling over workers with enforced disciplinary action. This doesn't feel right to Señora Corazon.

Señora Corazon is especially magnificent at bringing frontline workers back into balance when necessary. While she doesn't always hit the mark, she responds to her own errors and negative thoughts by redirecting her focus to what's great and right in the moment. Like the Nurtured Heart® Warriors Team, Señora Corazon has blossomed into a brilliant butterfly—but she's the most brilliant of them all.

Imagine It...

Let's pause for a moment. Please indulge me! Stop and take a deep breath. Imagine how magnificent it would feel to be wrapped in gold and silk. Embrace and savor this vision in your heart. Who wouldn't shine when bathed in gold and supported by the strength and softness of silk—when bathed in recognition and appreciation?

Continue to breathe this in as you read on.

Why Caterpillars and Butterflies?

Anyone who watches a caterpillar for any length of time knows that its main driving force in life is its appetite. It has an intense need to obtain as much nourishment as possible

> There is nothing in a caterpillar that tells us it's going to be a butterfly.
>
> —*Buckminster Fuller (1895–1983), inventor and architect*

to prepare for transformation. Caterpillars eat constantly—and they can't eat just anything. Each breed of caterpillar needs a different food in abundance in order to change and grow into a magnificent butterfly.

Similarly, we human beings require a huge amount of nutrition to grow and transform—but not the caloric kind (most of us get too much of that). We thrive most when we receive abundant spiritual and psychological nutrition in the form of love and positive relationship—just like the relationships cultivated between the Nurtured Heart® Warriors team and Isabella.

> *Our appetites for this kind of positive relationship exist just as much in the workplace as they do in any other realm of life.*

In preparation for metamorphosis, the caterpillar weaves a silken chrysalis—a word derived from the Greek word for gold. It demonstrates that while change is inevitable, it doesn't have to be painful. For us humans, positive relationship helps us to relax into transformation. It gives us the hope, faith, and sense of self-worth we require to keep morphing into greater and greater versions of ourselves. And this is what makes a workplace really golden: employees who already see themselves as successful and who genuinely want to build further success.

Butterflies are regarded as symbols of peace, happiness, and fidelity. In various cultures, butterflies have been symbolic of resurrection, the soul, eternal life, young love, transition, lightness, and beauty. They have been called "flowers that fly." In central Asia, Aztec Mexico, New Zealand, and Zaire, as well as in Christian mythology, the butterfly is considered a symbol of the soul. In Greek myth, Psyche (the Greek word for "soul") is symbolized by a butterfly. Ancient Christian tombs often included a depiction of a butterfly; Christ has been illustrated holding a butterfly in many works of art.

The caterpillar unquestioningly enters into transformation. Her body and her environment change in shocking ways as she follows her destiny. The butterfly's transformation is a fitting symbol for the life journey of the human being. Hopefully, the twists, turns, setbacks, and successes we experience all contribute to morphing us into what symbolism writer Avia Venefica calls "ever-finer beings."

As she goes into the dark night of metamorphosis to emerge completely transformed, she exemplifies trust and hope—a model for transformation for those who are held back from becoming their greatest selves by fear or uncertainty.

As our caterpillar selves transform into butterfly selves we realize that, contrary to what Buckminster Fuller said about caterpillars and butterflies, our butterfly selves—our qualities of greatness—were in us all along. That butterfly-ness was in our DNA just as butterfly-ness is in the DNA of the caterpillar. The metamorphosis is just about changing the expression of what we have always possessed.

And so the story goes…

Monday Morning

Isabella is due into work at 9:00 a.m. She arrives around 8:45 a.m. As she passes the coffee room, Ms. Canon—who is filling her cup—says brightly, "Good morning, Isabella! I see that you're here early. We cannot thank you enough for getting to work on time and for not being late! What a great role model to the rest of our team." "Thank you for that!" says Isabella as she begins her day feeling golden.

Positivity Pulse

Justice arrives shortly after Isabella—at 8:50. He's very conscientious about time. Usually, he arrives early enough at work to take care of any personal needs before diving into work promptly at 9:00. While walking into the building, he passes by his supervisor, Mr. Silencio—who barely acknowledges his existence, giving little more than a brief, unsmiling glance. Justice starts out his day with low energy.

Creative Recognitions, Inc.

Shortly into what appears to be a hectic Monday morning, Isabella is at her desk, managing a multitude of tasks. While passing by, Mr. Kodak says, "Good morning, Isabella. I notice how you're multitasking and getting so much accomplished! Quite impressive!"

Isabella thinks to herself what great bosses she has and how fortunate she is to have them. She feels a sense of

Positivity Pulse

connectedness deep within herself and a confidence regarding her work performance. As Isabella is nourished by her bosses, she begins to grow more golden stripes, taking on a burnished golden glow. She feels herself brimming over with creative ideas for completing the team's new project, and she can't wait to get started on the next phase.

On the other side of the office, Mr. Moody notices Justice working feverishly at his desk. "Good job, Justice!" he says as he walks by. Justice pauses for a moment. While it feels good to be told he's doing a good job, he wonders: *What am I doing well, exactly?* Although he's grateful not to have been the target of one of Mr. Moody's legendary bad-mood-induced jabs, he doesn't feel like he has been nourished by what has been said to him. Justice considers following Mr. Moody to ask him what exactly he has been doing right, but quickly changes his mind. Mr. Moody is not particularly approachable. Sometimes, when Justice asks for guidance, assistance, or support, he is met— often, without warning— with one of Mr. Moody's marvelous moods. Brushing off his thoughts, Justice goes back to his work. There is no luster in his being. His gold stripes are barely visible.

Positivity Pulse

As it gets closer to lunch hour, Mrs. Polaroid approaches Isabella to discuss the arrangements for the afternoon meeting with the CEO, Señora Corazon. Isabella is more than well prepared. She has achieved her goal of having everything organized and confirmed prior to taking her lunch break. Impressed, Mrs. Polaroid happily tells Isabella, "You are so incredibly organized, Isabella! I notice how hard you are always working. This shows us what a team player you are. You're demonstrating valuable leadership skills. Thank you for all you do for us!"

Creative Recognitions, Inc.

Isabella is more lustrous than ever. Her golden stripes grow exponentially; she shines with radiance.

Conversely, Justice begins to move at a snail's pace. When he's not completely unfocused, he wonders why he is at this job. Sometimes he feels invisible. He is falling behind on some of his deadlines and is quickly becoming more and more distracted. He wonders what his girlfriend is doing and decides to send her a text. She texts back right away. Back and forth the texts fly. This is not the first time that Justice has broken the rule of not using his personal cell phone in the workplace, but when Mr. Silencio walks by and notices him doing this, he doesn't say anything. Then, he's also caught by Mr. Moody, who calls him out. "It's just a quick message," Justice tells him. "Oh, OK. No problem," Mr. Moody replies, and keeps walking.

And then, Mrs. Crabtree catches him texting. The subsequent lecture goes on and on and on: "How many times do we need to remind you, Justice, that the use of personal cell phones is not permitted on the company's time? I cannot understand why this is so challenging for you! As it is, I can clearly see that you've fallen behind for our deadline for this afternoon's meeting with Señora Corazon. I am sorry, Justice, but we are going to have to have a discussion about this *right now!* Let's go into my office to discuss this matter. And we also have to call Human Resources. I just cannot believe we have to address this again and again, Justice. When will it end? Now I have to spend all this time with you because you insist on using your cell phone to conduct personal business at work!" Even as Mrs. Crabtree waxes poetic about Justice's misdeeds, Justice barely hears a word of it.

Positivity Pulse

After Mrs. Crabtree has finished with him, Justice slithers back into his cubicle. He feels like an empty shell. His faint gold stripes are quickly disappearing. He longs for 5:00 p.m. to arrive. Maybe he could go home sick? Yes—he could tell Mrs. Crabtree that he was trying to get his girlfriend to make him a doctor's appointment because he hasn't been feeling well. He could make up a story and just go home early.

Wait, he thinks. *If I go home now, I'll never make that deadline. I've got to get back to work. And it's only Monday.* Deflated, faded, he turns back to his work.

Creative Recognitions, Inc.

At lunch, Justice and Isabella sit down in the break room. Justice briefly greets Isabella, but he doesn't feel like chatting because he feels jealousy toward her. She looks radiant. Her excitement about her current project, Project Transformation, is palpable. She can barely contain her enthusiasm; clearly, she's yearning to get back to work as soon as she finishes her lunch.

Justice has really enjoyed working with Isabella and respects her a great deal. They've had a close collegial relationship. But today, he's in no mood for all her joy and positive energy. In fact, he's in no mood to be around anyone. Isabella asks him what's wrong.

"I got in trouble for texting with my girlfriend," he tells her. "Mrs. Crabtree brought me into her office and yelled at me for a good ten minutes. I was in such a bad mood, I almost faked being sick so I could go home."

"But you decided to stay and keep working," Isabella tells him brightly. "That's real commitment. That's perseverance."

Unmoved by Isabella's positivity—really, he's only half listening—Justice says, "I guess I got what I deserved." He finishes his lunch and trudges back to his desk. Maybe he isn't physically sick, but he's sick internally. He's leaking energy, and he can't figure out how to shake this feeling of being disconnected from his co-workers and bosses.

Nourishment for Transformation

Children and adolescents develop in stages; so do employees, teams, and students. Employees go through stages of development in the workplace. Some research posits that it takes a new employee six months to acclimate and assimilate in his or her new environment. Consider the more seasoned employees along a trajectory—a golden path—that also requires ongoing nutrition to support flourishing mind, body, and spirit.

Most of us don't see the caterpillar as stunning

Theoretically, from the day a person steps foot into your workplace, he or she is beginning in the earliest stages of development in your organization. With each new employee, you have a golden opportunity to nourish him or her with all of the nutrients required for positive growth and change.

or graceful. But in essence, the caterpillar is the spirit form of the butterfly. Only if that spirit is nurtured during the caterpillar stage can it transform and grace us with its intricacy, brilliance, and beauty.

When we notice, in detail, what staff or students do right, we are supporting their metamorphosis—their transformation into a human being who is flourishing rather than enduring.

Butterflies, once transformed, require continued nourishment to flourish. Many prefer the sweet taste of nectar. And all staff, even executive team members, need continuous nourishment. They too thrive better when the nutrition offered is sweet (like the nutrition Isabella receives) rather than bitter (like the nutrition Justice received from Mrs. Crabtree).

At Creative Recognitions, Inc., transformation occurs when recognition and appreciation are offered instead of negativity. This likely makes intuitive sense to you. It points the way down a road that an employee like Justice feels compelled to follow to the consternation of those who wish he'd make different choices.

Positive recognitions are energizing. Negativity saps energy, but it also has a way of energizing the recipient to make more negative choices.

Negativity doesn't get us what we want as leaders. Even when it does, the rewards tend to be short-lived and to create problems that have to be dealt with later: contentious relationships, hurt feelings, and choices to go against policy or procedure. Staff best develop toward success when they are "fed" with detailed positive feedback.

Positivity Pulse

Administratively & organizationally, this kind of environment increases productivity, creates positive workplaces, and energizes brilliance and teamwork. Employees feel valued. They want to come to work and do their absolute best.

Human beings can get stuck too when forced to do without positive social, emotional, and intellectual interrelationships.

This pulse of positivity works best when balanced with a kind of "tough love" where noncompliance, conflicts, and negative energy are addressed head on with total consistency.

Most of us get that a positive road is better for all, but few know how to achieve a consistent flow of honest, heartfelt, positive recognition and appreciation—the psychological and spiritual nutrition that best supports employees in being the best they can be.

When the caterpillar cannot access the nutrients it requires to transform, it slows down and gets stuck in that stage. Lack of positive relationship can cause us to become downtrodden, depressed, doubtful, worried, angry, or isolated.

Your most important role as a leader is to provide nourishment at every level of the workplace. When that role is fulfilled, employees thrive and the entire organization flourishes. Problems are dealt with promptly and efficiently, and the next step is back into greatness.

In a sense, you're also the mother butterfly (even if you're the wrong gender for motherhood, you can still play this symbolic role) who has found the ideal place for her caterpillars to flourish, enabling them to do so rather independently. Once you have placed those caterpillars just so and given them high-quality nutrition for a while, they become more able to flourish and transform on their own.

Now, let's head back to Creative Recognitions, Inc., in time for an important meeting…

Project Transformation Meeting: Monday, 2:00 p.m. Location: Main Conference Room

Señora Corazon waits patiently for her management teams and their team members to join her in the main conference room. As she waits, she thinks: *Project Transformation is crucial to the ongoing development of the company. In today's market, having the ability to be dynamic and to change with the many challenges with which we are faced gives us an edge. It's what keeps our company in business.* She sets her intention to observe, in her teams, whose dynamism and flexibility seem to be coming through strongly and whose seem to be flagging. She wants to discover what makes the difference between employees who are energized and flourishing and those who are disengaged, discontented, and languishing.

As everyone arrives, she immediately observes that members of the Nurtured Heart® Warriors team—both frontline and management—are bursting with ideas. They seem genuinely happy to see one another. Frontline workers are even happy to see their team leaders, Mr. Kodak, Mrs. Polaroid, and Ms. Canon. Señora Corazon feels the pleasure of watching them interact with one another with mutual respect. In the chatter before the meeting begins, these team members engage in a reciprocal exchange where they are all learning, growing, and transforming.

As the other team members convene, Señora Corazon notices an astonishing disparity. Members of Team Chrysalis sit quietly and seem disengaged. "These meetings are such a waste of time," one team member mutters.

As he hurries in from his desk, Justice notices how Isabella and her team members all have a golden, glowing look. He wonders why his team members are so dull and negative. He thinks that the other team must have a secret weapon—something that is uniting them in fast, joyful movement toward project completion.

Señora Corazon sees this polarity of negativity and positivity. In her mind, she mounts a critical analysis of what is happening under her leadership: *Half of my employees are spilling over with abundant intellect and energy and amazing ideas. Half of them are presenting brilliantly and transforming right before my eyes. Others are observably downtrodden, sullen, disengaged, and even angry. Some seem very connected to each other; others seem disenfranchised.*

Señora Corazon is certain of one thing: that all of her managers and team members are amazing. She wouldn't trade in a single one. Some are shining, while others are stuck, unable to transform. Project Transformation will not work for their company if only half of the employees make it.

As she starts the meeting, Señora Corazon notices how the members of Team Chrysalis respond as she begins to do what comes naturally to her: recognizing her employees' outstanding contribution in active, experiential, and proactive ways. She notices how Justice instantly begins to glimmer when she notices him making a real effort to stay focused in the meeting. She knows Justice has a challenge with this. She says, "I need everyone to bring all of their attention and energy to every meeting. Justice is setting the example today—he's completely

focused, keeping his eyes on me as I present to you all. Thank you, Justice!"

The leaders of Team Chrysalis respond with warmth when their CEO makes a point of acknowledging their successes in detail—even when those successes are small ones. Even when they're just doing what they're supposed to be doing, this visionary CEO sees that they could be making other choices to do what they *aren't* supposed to be doing, and calls them on their good choices out loud where everyone can hear.

It quickly becomes clear that the pulse of positivity has remarkable effects—not only on those who had thus far been steeped in negativity, but also on team members who were already thriving. Señora Corazon herself feels the benefit of modeling positivity, and when the meeting adjourns, everyone's in high spirits. They return to their work with renewed enthusiasm. Everyone's just a little more golden.

"Time to find a way to bring this pulse of positivity into our whole workplace," Señora Corazon muses to her assistant in the meeting's aftermath.

"Hmm. I like the sound of that," her assistant answers. "The Positivity Pulse!"

"Yes!" Señora Corazon says with characteristic passion. "Commence Operation Positivity Pulse!"

The Positivity Pulse Begins to Beat!

Señora Corazon realizes that she has the responsibility and the power to change things for employees who have felt detached, disaffected, and steeped in negativity. She also sees that the transformation she wants to make in her own workplace will bring great clarity to the work her company does to help others transform their workplaces.

First, she decides to spend several days simply noticing what is happening under her leadership. Sometimes, worried and doubtful thoughts come up. *Can I really transform my workplace? Can I really create this vision I imagine where positivity is the common denominator to all we do? What if I fail?* She finds, however, that by quickly "resetting" herself back to the project of getting this Positivity Pulse to work in her organization, she finds herself right back in the flow of her intensity, from which she can move forth with zeal and passion.

Over the next two days, she commits herself to assessing the pulse in her company. She notices the different styles of her six managers from the Nurtured Heart® Warriors Team and Team Chrysalis.

Mr. Kodak, Mrs. Polaroid, and Ms. Canon are often heard relating to their team members. They are all working and producing, but their relationships stand out as most meaningful. An outsider coming into their work space is likely to want to join them. When conflict comes up, they unceremoniously address it and work through it swiftly. These managers relate to one another in a manner that feels like a celebration.

Conversely, Team Chrysalis is leaking energy. They barely relate to one another unless something goes wrong. The frontline workers are visibly deflated. Mr. Moody, Mrs. Crabtree, and Mr. Silencio collectively have an apparent and resounding *negative* pulse! Clearly, this management team does not seem to notice the greatness of their team members—or even the greatness they themselves possess. But Señora Corazon finds that if she walks through their work station and notices Justice or the others in positive ways, they respond with golden brilliance.

Señora Corazon notices how the positivity and collegiality evident between leaders of the Nurtured Heart® Warriors team seems to be completely missing from Team Chrysalis. Team leaders seem constantly stressed, even frenzied. They bark orders and struggle and push to meet deadlines.

There's no doubt in Senora Corazon's mind that Team Chrysalis managers require an entire makeover. Their negative energy is leaking onto their frontline workers. She knows that Mr. Moody, Mrs. Crabtree, and Mr. Silencio are all capable and have great hearts. With a few tools, she reasons, they'll be able to shift from negativity to positivity, which will enable them to manage their staff more effectively—to nurture their greatness. And to determine what those tools would be, she could use the approach of the Nurtured Heart® Warriors Team.

Señora Corazon also realizes that she will have to fearlessly, relentlessly model this approach herself. She knows that if she copies Mr. Kodak, Mrs. Polaroid, and Ms. Canon precisely, Project Transformation will be a smashing success that will take her company to a new level of greatness.

Although she is naturally in alignment with the Nurtured Heart® Team's approach, she has to be honest and evaluate herself in this process. She too has to make some changes. She's fantastic at creatively recognizing everyone and at maintaining order and compliance, but she also sees that Team Chrysalis remains stuck. She'll have to kick it up a few notches by amplifying her recognitions and appreciation.

She gathers her management teams together for an urgent meeting. Once everyone has arrived, she tells them: "All of you know that the Nurtured Heart® Team is closer to metamorphosis than Team Chrysalis. If we are all going to come together to complete Project Transformation on time, some of us will need to change our ways. Starting now, we're all going to learn from the Nurtured Heart® Team about how we can relate to one another more effectively and with greater positivity. We're going to bring their Positivity Pulse to our entire organization."

At first, protests erupt from Team Chrysalis. There are

excuses; there's finger-pointing and blaming. But Señora Corazon holds fast to both her edict and her positivity. Refusing to give the negativity any energy, she simply says, "This is how things are going to be. You can deviate from the plan if you want, but your performance evaluations will be negatively affected by that choice."

Eventually, everyone gets on board—some less willingly than others. Over time, both leadership teams observe and imitate the ways in which the Nurtured Heart® Warriors Team communicates and leads. They even spend one-on-one time with these leaders to find out more about their *internal dialogues*—how they talk to and nurture themselves. As Team Chrysalis begins to play around with these new tools, workers like Justice begin to enjoy coming to work. They start to see that they are valued and that they have much to offer. They begin to pick up the very tools their supervisors are learning. Creative Recognitions, Inc., is transformed.

About the Author
Sherry A. Blair

As CEO of Sherry Blair Institute For Inspirational Change, Sherry A. Blair inspires and motivates others by applying and encouraging Positive Psychology. She uses her skills to teach others how to build effective teams, and use non-violent communication to achieve results and resolve conflict. Teaching others to speak from their hearts is a key constituent of the work she does. Sherry is one of the first 300 in the world to be trained by Dr. Martin Seligman in his 2003 Vanguard Training, Authentic Happiness Positive Psychology Coaching Program.

Sherry graduated Rutgers University with a Bachelor of Arts in Psychology and Women's Studies. She went on to obtain her Master of Science in Social Work with a concentration in Policy Analysis and International Social Welfare at Columbia University. Dually mastered in Industrial and Organizational Psychology, Sherry also holds a Doctorate of Philosophy in Management, supporting her vision to make change at the macro level in leadership and management.

She is an Advanced Trainer/Certified Nurtured Heart® Specialist and has served on the Ethics & Global Summit Committees for Howard Glasser and the Nurtured Heart Approach®, a transformational approach that changes lives. She is also a Licensed Practitioner through The iOpener Institute in The Science of Happiness. She is the author of *The Positivity Pulse: Transforming Your Workplace* and a recent contributor to *Roadmap to Success: America's Top Intellectual Minds Map Out Successful Business Strategies* with Ken Blanchard and Deepak Chopra. She has also just released books for children and teens to ignite flourishing and leadership in the formative years, and *Optimize: 7 Simple Steps to Nurturing Your Heart* is coming soon.

To inquire about coaching, consulting, training, and development services in your organization contact us: info@SherryBlairInstitute.com.

Creative Recognitions, Inc. is the fable that originally was published in *The Positivity Pulse: Transforming Your Workplace* as Chapter One by Sherry Blair with Melissa Lynn Block.

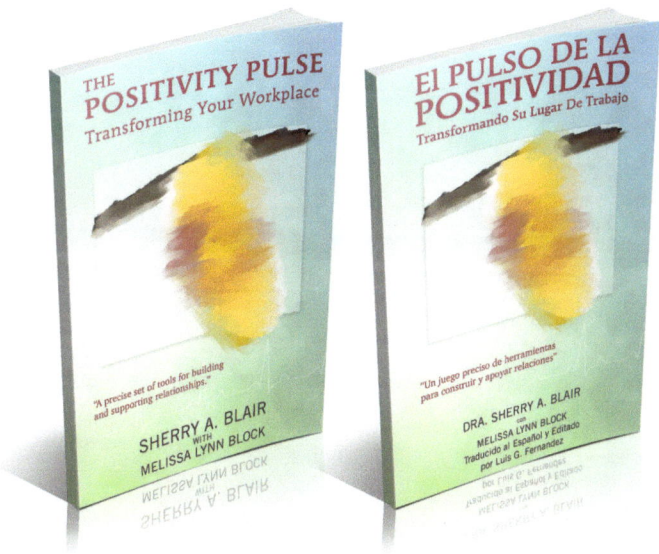

SherryBlairInstitute.com

www.ingramcontent.com/pod-product-compliance
Lightning Source LLC
Chambersburg PA
CBHW040919180526
45159CB00002BA/538